W9-AUD-650

ISN'T GOD GREAT!

Illustrated by Amelia Rosato

Chariot Books™
David C. Cook Publishing Co.
850 North Grove Avenue, Elgin, Illinois 60120

He is higher than the highest mountain.

Deeper than the ocean bed.

He is stronger than

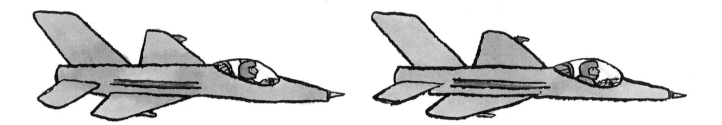

the biggest army.

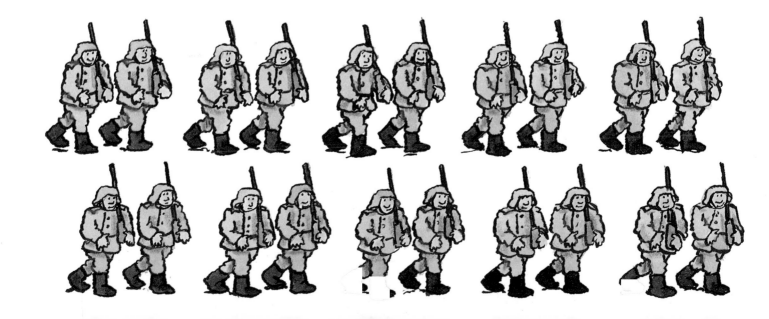

Gentler than
the softest touch.

He's older than
the dinosaurs.

Wiser than the philosophers.

More faithful than
a trusting dog.

Closer than my closest friend.

Bigger than the universe.

But He cares for
the smallest blade of grass.

Isn't He great?!

Chariot Books™ is an imprint of David C. Cook Publishing Co.
David C. Cook Publishing Co., Elgin, Illinois 60120
David C. Cook Publishing Co., Weston, Ontario

Isn't God Great!

First published in the UK by Hunt & Thorpe 1992
© Hunt & Thorpe 1992
Text © Hamish Trump 1992
Illustrations © Amelia Rosato 1992

First printing, 1992
96 95 94 93 92 5 4 3 2 1
ISBN 0-7814-0008-2

All rights reserved.
No part of this publication may be reproduced, stored in a retrieval system, or
transmitted in any form or by any means, electronic, mechanical, photocopying,
recording or otherwise, without the prior permission of the publisher.

Printed in Singapore.